Kids Best Jokes

Callan
Jones

49 marine
Terace Blyth
Northuberland
Post code
ne2t 2Jp

Kids' Best Jokes

Compiled by Karen King
Illustrated by Stuart Trotter

Hippo Books
Scholastic Publications Limited
London

Scholastic Publications Ltd.,
10 Earlham Street, London WC2H 9RX, UK

Scholastic Inc.,
730 Broadway, New York, NY 10003, USA

Scholastic Tab Publications Ltd.,
123 Newkirk Road, Richmond Hill,
Ontario L4C 3G5, Canada

Ashton Scholastic Pty Ltd.,
P O Box 579, Gosford, New South Wales,
Australia

Ashton Scholastic Ltd.,
165 Marua Road, Panmure, Auckland 6,
New Zealand

Text copyright © Scholastic Publications Ltd., 1990
Illustrations copyright © Stuart Trotter, 1990

First published by Scholastic Publications Ltd., 1990

ISBN 0 590 76281 8

All rights reserved

Typeset by AKM Associates (UK) Ltd., Southall, London
Made and printed by Cox & Wyman, Reading, Berks

10 9 8 7 6 5 4 3 2 1

This book is sold subject to the condition that it shall not, by way of trade or otherwise be lent, resold, hired out, or otherwise circulated without the publisher's prior consent in any form of binding or cover other than that in which it is published and without a similar condition, including this condition, being imposed upon the subsequent purchaser.

CONTENTS

Introduction	7
Best Jokes	9
The School Outing	14
Feline Fun	16
It's A-moo-sing!	17
News Flash	18
Nutty Knowledge	20
Classroom Chuckles	24
It's Riddliculous!	29
Lost and Found	32
What Did . . .?	33
Wacky Waiters	36
Did You Hear the One About . . .?	38
Knock, Knock!	41
Memory Test	49
Cross-Words	49
What a Laugh!	51
Animal Crackers	55
Cops n' Robbers	58
I Say, I Say, I Say . . .	60
How Clever Are You?	63
Can You Guess . . .?	65
Brainteasers	67
What's the Name?	69

Jumbo Jokes	71
Something Fishy	72
It's Quackers	74
Did You Know . . .?	75
Cheeky Kids	77
Jungle Jinks	79
Stan and Clive	81
Incredible Insects	83
Silly Sports	85
Doctor, Doctor . . .	86
Quick Riddles	90
Horror Howlers	96
Spot the Difference	101
Mummy, Mummy . . .	102
Farmyard Fun	104
Ridiculous Rhymes	108
And Finally . . .	110

INTRODUCTION

Here at Hippo we like to laugh; we like to laugh so much, that a short while ago we came up with this brilliant idea. "Let's get our readers to send in all their favourite jokes and make them into a book!"

We laughed a lot when the first post bag came. We laughed quite a lot when the second bag came. We laughed a lot less when the next two came; and when the postman had crawled back and forwards with ten heavy bags, we started to get a bit worried. Maybe KID'S BEST JOKES wasn't such a great idea after all!

We emptied every single sack, opened every single letter, read every single joke and laughed loudly – every so often (some jokes aren't very funny when you've read them a hundred times)!

Loads of people sent in the joke about the deer with no eyes, *loads* of people sent in the one about playing cards in the jungle... *loads* of people sent in with nearly every joke in the book... Of course, you'll howl with laughter at every single one – after all, *you* don't have to read them a hundred times!

With so many entries to choose from, picking the winners was not an easy job! The *Best Jokes* at the beginning of the book are the ones that were the most unusual. We hope you like them.

Thanks to everyone who entered our competition. It's a shame we can't send you all a prize but, luckily for us, there were just too many of you!

BEST JOKES

Son: "How much pocket money can I have, Dad?"
Dad: "Fifty pence a week."
Son: "What, only fifty pence a week? That's an insult!"
Dad: "I'll pay you monthly then, so you don't get insulted so much."

(Sent by: Ania Majewski, Southgate, London.)

Mum: "Come on, John, eat up your breakfast or you'll be late for school."
John: "I don't want to go to school. The teachers don't like me, the children don't like me, even the caretaker doesn't like me."
Mum: "That may be so, but you still have to go to school."
John: "Why?"
Mum: "Because you're the headmaster."

(Sent by: Amelia Whittaker, Berwickshire, Scotland.)

A man was telling his friend what happened to his budgie. "I was filling my cigarette lighter when I dropped some fuel, and the budgie flew down and sipped it up. Then it zoomed up the stairs, twirled twice in the bathroom, zoomed back down again, flew over to the sink and stopped dead."

"Was it dead?" asked his friend.

"No," said the man. "It had just run out of petrol."

(Sent by: Ryan Campbell, Kincardine by Alloe, Clacks, Scotland.)

Headmaster: "This is the third time I've had to cane you this week, Smithers. What have you got to say about that?"
Smithers: "Thank goodness it's Friday!"

(Sent by: Simon Barclay, Edinburgh, Scotland.)

Why are barbers never late for work?
Because they know all the short cuts.

(Sent by: Christopher Dean, Aylesford, Kent.)

Two mountain climbers were climbing Mount Everest. The first climber had a fall and broke both his legs and arms, so he had to hold the rope in his mouth whilst the second climber pulled him up the mountain. Somehow they managed to struggle like this until they were almost at the top of the mountain.

"We're nearly there. Are you okay?" the second climber called.

The first one shouted, "Yeeeeees . . . . Crunch!"

(Sent by: Vicki Snodgrass, Launceston, Cornwall.)

The Proud Lion

There was once a lion who was very proud. One day, he went up to a giraffe and roared, "Who is the king of the jungle?"

"You are, O King," replied the giraffe.

The lion was very pleased and strutted off through the jungle. Soon he came to a zebra drinking at a water hole. "Who is the king of the jungle?" he roared.

"You are, O King," said the zebra.

The lion was very pleased and walked off again. Soon he met a monkey and roared, "Who is king of the jungle?"

"You are, O King," said the monkey. And the lion trotted off, feeling very pleased with himself.

Next, the lion came to an elephant and roared again, "Who is the king of the jungle?"

The elephant picked the lion up with his trunk, threw him up into the air, jumped on him, then threw him into the river.

When the lion climbed out he said, "All right, all right, there's no need to act like that, just because you don't know the answer."

(Sent by: James Woodhead, Aberdeen, Scotland.)

Where do you find giant snails?
On the end of giant's fingers.

(Sent by: David Meadows, Argyllshire, Scotland.)

What do you get if you cross a clock with a joker?
A laugh a minute.

(Sent by: Rebecca Featherstone, Canterbury, Kent.)

What do you get if you cross a mouse with a bar of soap?
Bubble and squeak.

(Sent by: Jasmail Dhillon, Southall, Middlesex.)

THE SCHOOL OUTING

Teacher: "This year's class outing will be to the seaside."
Class: "Hooray!"
Teacher: "It will cost £40."
Class: "Boo!"
Teacher: "By train or £1.50 by coach."
Class: "Hooray!"
Teacher: "The headmaster will be coming."
Class: "Boo!"
Teacher: "To see us off."
Class: "Hooray!"
Teacher: "The weather will be wet and windy."
Class: "Boo!"
Teacher: "In Russia and warm and sunny in Britain."
Class: "Hooray!"

Teacher: "There will be no swimming."
Class: "Boo!"
Teacher: "Until we get there."
Class: "Hooray!"
Teacher: "Lunch will be boiled fish and cabbage."
Class: "Boo!"
Teacher: "For me and crisps, Coke and Smarties for you."
Class: "Hooray!"
Teacher: "There will be a visit to the museum."
Class: "Boo!"
Teacher: "Or if preferred, to the funfair."
Class: "Hooray!"
Teacher: "But we must be back at 12 o'clock."
Class: "Boo!"
Teacher: "Midnight!"
Class: "Hooray!"

FELINE FUN

Where do cats keep their savings?
The Tabby National.

Why don't cats shave?
Because eight out of ten cats prefer whiskers.

What do cats like for breakfast?
Mice Krispies.

What do you get if you cross a cat with a lemon?
A sourpuss.

What do cats read on Sundays?
Mews of the World.

John: "There were ten cats on a boat, one jumped off and none were left."
Bill: "How's that?"
John: "They were all copycats."

What happened to the cat that swallowed a ball of wool?
She had mittens.

Tabby Cat: "How did you get on in the milk-drinking contest?"
Black Cat: "I won by six laps."

How do you get milk from a cat?
Take away its saucer.

What did the dog say to the cat?
Woof! Woof! (of course)

IT'S A-MOO-SING!

Why do cows have bells?
Because their horns don't work.

What does a cow with hiccups give you?
A milk shake.

Where do cows go for an evening out?
To the moo-vies.

What game do cows like to play?
Moo-sical chairs.

Where do cows go for their holidays?
Moo York.

What do you call an Arctic cow?
An Eskimoo.

How do farmers count their cows?
They use cowculators.

What do you get if you sit under a cow?
A pat on the head.

NEWS FLASH

Twenty packets of paste have been stolen from the D.I.Y. store. Police say it was a stick-up job.

Ten chocolate fingers have been taken from the biscuit factory. Police say they are looking for someone with chocolate hands.

A farmer in Yorkshire has had eleven of his twelve deer stolen. Police say he is now down to his last buck.

An aeroplane landed on the roof of a man's house in London late last night. Evidently he'd left his landing light on.

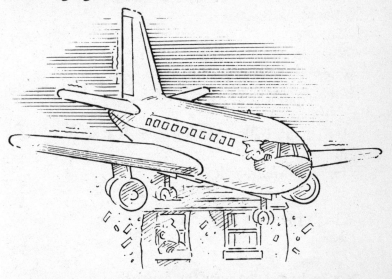

The Post Office has asked people to stop sending telegrams to Washington. They would like to remind the public that he's dead.

Doctors today warned against people trying to write on an empty stomach—they advise using paper instead.

NUTTY KNOWLEDGE

What do you call a road with diamonds down the middle?
A jewel carriageway.

Which town in Britain makes terrible sandwiches?
Oldham.

Where do hamsters come from?
Hamsterdam.

How many balls of string does it take to reach Jupiter?
One, if it's long enough.

What's the coldest country in the world?
Chile.

Which bus sailed over the ocean?
Columbus.

Why do birds fly south in winter?
Because it's too far to walk.

What kind of stars are dangerous?
Shooting stars.

Which is heavier, a full moon or a half moon?
A half moon, because a full moon is lighter.

How was the Roman Empire cut in half?
With a pair of Caesars.

What did Noah use to light his ark?
Floodlights.

Who was the fastest runner in the world?
Adam. He was first in the human race.

Who invented fire?
A bright spark.

Which building has the most storeys?
The library.

When did only 3 vowels exist?
Before U and I were born.

Who invented fractions?
Henry 1/8.

What is an ig?
An Eskimo's house that has no loo.

When does Friday come before Thursday?
In the dictionary.

Why did Robin Hood only steal from the rich?
Because the poor had nothing worth stealing.

What happens when you throw a green stone in the Red Sea?
It gets wet.

What do you get if you cross an egg white with gun powder?
Boom-meringue.

What begins with a P and ends with an E and has thousands and thousands of letters?
The Post Office.

What's the laziest mountain in the world?
Mount Ever-rest.

CLASSROOM CHUCKLES

Teacher: "Which family does the octopus belong to?"
Jenny: "No one in our street, Sir."

Teacher: "David! Didn't you hear me calling you?"
David: "Yes Sir, but yesterday you told me not to answer back."

Teacher: "Mason, what is the outer part of a tree called?"
Mason: "I don't know, Sir."
Teacher: "Bark, boy, bark!"
Mason: "Woof! Woof!"

Teacher: "Now, Susie, how much is five and five?"

Susie: "Nine, Miss."
Teacher: "Wrong. It's ten."
Susie: "It can't be. You told me yesterday that six and four made ten!"

Teacher: "What is the opposite of minimum?"
Smart Alec: "Minidad!"

Teacher: "Who can tell me where the Andes are?"
Angie: "On the end of my armies!"

John: "Please Sir, would you punish me for something I haven't done?"
Teacher: "Good heavens, of course not!"
John: "Thank goodness for that. I haven't done my homework."

Little Boy: "Mummy, I think my teacher loves me!"
Mother: "Why, dear?"
Little Boy: "She keeps putting kisses in my book!"

Mother: "How were the exam questions today, Michael?"
Michael: "The questions were okay, it was the answers I had trouble with!"

Father: "Betty, I want you to have something I never had at school."
Betty: "What's that? Good results?"

Teacher: "What's that book you're reading, Stevens?"
Stevens: "It's the Dinosaur Joke Book, Sir."
Teacher: "Put it away; this is a history lesson."
Stevens: "But, Sir, this book is pre-hysterical!"

A boy came out of school looking upset. "I told my teacher that my name is Arthur Mickey Brown but he said he's just going to call me Arthur Brown," he told his mother.

"What's wrong with that?" she asked.

"I don't like the Mickey being taken out of my name!" the boy replied.

Teacher: "Right, Jones, spell blind pig."
Jones: "B–l–n–d–p–g."
Teacher: "But what about the I's?"
Jones: "Please Sir, a blind pig doesn't have any eyes!"

Teacher: "What's your name?"
Pupil: "Henry."
Teacher: "Say Sir."
Pupil: "Okay. Sir Henry."

Teacher: "Who can tell me two days of the week beginning with T?"
Bright Spark: "Me, Miss. Today and Tomorrow!"

Headmaster: "Ah, Anne, you missed school yesterday, didn't you?"
Anne: "Not a bit, Sir."

Teacher: "Mary, why are you late again?"
Mary: "Sorry, Sir. I started out early and was walking along the High Street when I saw this sign that said 'Go Slow,' so I did."

Father: "Did you get a good place in your exams, Son?"
Son: "Yes, Dad, I sat right by the radiator."

"I won a prize at school today, Mummy," said little Bernard. "The teacher asked how many legs an elephant has, so I said three."

"Three!" exclaimed his mother. "Then how on earth did you win the prize?"

"I was the closest," replied Bernard.

A little girl opened the door to her teacher. "Are your parents in?" asked the teacher.

The little girl shook her head. "They was in but now they is out," she replied.

"They WAS in but now they IS out!" exclaimed the teacher. "Where's your grammar?"

"In the front room watching the telly," the little girl told her.

"I want you all to watch this experiment very carefully," the teacher told his class. He put two worms in a glass of water and they wriggled about quite happily. Then he put two worms in a glass of whisky. These worms curled up and died. "Now, children, what do we learn from this?" asked the teacher.

One bright spark put up his hand and said, "Please Sir, if you have worms, drink whisky."

IT'S RIDDLICULOUS!

Why is a leg of pork like an old radio?
You get crackling from both.

What do jelly babies wear when it's raining?
Gumboots.

What has an eye but can't see?
A needle.

What smells, has four wheels and flies?
A dustcart.

Why do koala bears carry their babies on their backs?
They can't push prams up trees.

What stays hot even if you put it in the fridge?
Mustard.

What's black and white and goes round and round?
A penguin in a revolving door.

What wears a coat all winter and pants all summer?
A dog.

What's the best thing to put in a pie?
Your teeth.

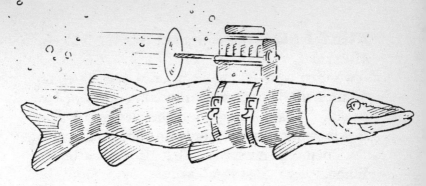

What goes through the water at 100 miles per hour?
A motor pike.

How do you get freckles?
Sunbathe under a sieve.

What nuts can you hang pictures on?
Walnuts.

Why are rivers rich?
Because they have two banks.

What's red and goes beep, beep?
A strawberry in a traffic jam.

What runs but has no legs?
A tap.

What sort of bow is it impossible to tie?
A rainbow.

LOST AND FOUND

Two men were laying a carpet in a living-room. When half the room was finished they stopped for lunch. "That's funny. I made two sandwiches this morning, but I can only find one," said one of the men. "I must have left the other one at home."

After they'd eaten their lunch, the men carried on laying the carpet. When they'd finished, they noticed a big lump in the middle of the room and one of the men said, "Look, Bill, that must be your sandwich."

"It's okay, I'll fix it," said Bill. He fetched a mallet and bashed hard on the lump. "There, flat as a pancake," he said.

After they'd packed their things and were about to leave, Bill noticed a sandwich on the window-sill. "Hey, here's my sandwich," he said. "I wonder what that lump was?"

Just then the door opened and a sad-looking little boy came in. "Have you seen my teddy bear?" he asked, "I've looked everywhere and can't find it."

WHAT DID . . .?

What did the lollipop say to the boy?
"Hello, sucker."

What did the puddle say to the rain?
"Why don't you drop in some time?"

What did the dog say to the skeleton?
"I've got a bone to pick with you."

What did the bee say to the flower?
"Hello, Honey!"

What did the balloon say to the pin?
"Hiya, Buster."

What did the stick insect say to his friend?
"Stick around."

What did Mr Mouse say to Mrs Mouse?
"I love you, squeakheart."

What did the boy candle say to the girl candle?
"Let's go out together."

What did the traffic light say to the car?
"Don't look now, I'm changing."

What did the hat say to the scarf?
"You hang around and I'll go on ahead."

What did the big telephone say to the little telephone?
"You're too young to be engaged."

What did Hamlet say to the weightwatchers?
"Tubby or not tubby."

What did the envelope say to the stamp?
"Stick with me and we'll go places."

What did the big chimney say to the little chimney?
"You're too young to smoke."

What did the bus conductor say to the one-legged man?
"How are you getting on?"

What did the two salt–cellars say after they'd had a fight?
"Shake?"

What did one eye say to the other eye?
"Between you and me, something smells."

What did one flea say to another flea?
"Shall we walk or take a cat?"

What did one volcano say to another volcano?
"Don't blow your top."

What did the wolf say to the fur coat?
"Hello, darling."

What did the girl say to the banana?
"I'm going to skin you."

WACKY WAITERS

Customer: "Waiter, this crab has only one claw!"
Waiter: "It's been in a fight, Sir."
Customer: "In that case I'd rather have the winner."

Customer: "Waiter, why is this apple pie all smashed up?"
Waiter: "Well, Sir, you asked for a slice of apple pie and told me to step on it!"

Customer: "Waiter, is this a chicken or beef pie?"
Waiter: "What did you order, Sir?"

Customer: "Waiter, I want a really good meal. What do you recommend?"
Waiter: "Eat at another restaurant, Sir."

A gentleman dining at Crewe,
Found quite a large mouse in his stew.
The waiter said, "Don't shout
And wave it about,
Or the others will all want one too!"

What's the best way to see a flying saucer?
Trip up a waiter!

Chef: "I thought I told you to watch that pan of water to see when it boiled."
Trainee: "I did watch it—it boiled over at 8.30."

Customer: "Waiter, have you got frog's legs?"
Waiter: "No Sir, it's just the way I walk!"

DID YOU HEAR THE ONE ABOUT...?

Did you hear about the man who got an electric shock?
He stood on a bun and a currant shot up his leg.

Did you hear about the wooden car?
It had wooden wheels, wooden windows and wooden go.

Did you hear the joke about the dustbin?
It's a load of rubbish.

Did you hear about the two flies playing football in a saucer?
They were practising for the cup.

Did you hear about the boy who worked in the clock factory?
He spent all day making faces.

Did you hear the joke about the butter?
I'd better not tell you–you might spread it.

Did you hear the joke about the high wall?
I'd better not tell you–you might not get over it.

Did you hear the joke about the lump of coal?
I'd better not tell you–it's too dirty.

Did you hear the joke about the bodysnatchers?
I'd better not tell you – you might get carried away.

Did you hear about the girl who dreamed she was eating a giant marshmallow?
When she woke up the next morning her pillow was gone.

Did you hear about the hyena who swallowed an oxo cube?
He made a laughing stock of himself.

Did you hear about the woman who washed her front doorstep?
She broke her washing machine.

Did you hear the joke about the empty house?
There was nothing in it.

Did you hear about the two peanuts walking down Piccadilly?
One was a-salted!

Did you hear about the actor who was so keen to play Long John Silver he had his leg cut off?
He still didn't get the part – it was the wrong leg!

KNOCK, KNOCK!

Knock, knock.
Who's there?
Either.
Either who?
Either you're deaf or your doorbell needs fixing.

Knock, knock.
Who's there?
Isabel.
Isabel who?
Isabel necessary on a bicycle?

Knock, knock.
Who's there?
Police.
Police who?
Police let me in; it's freezing out here!

Knock, knock.
Who's there?
Francis.
Francis who?
Francis across the English Channel.

Knock, knock.
Who's there?
Alex.
Alex who?
Alexplain later.

Knock, knock.
Who's there?
I, Senior.
I, Senior who?
I Senior kissing behind the garages.

Knock, knock.
Who's there?
Boo.
Boo who?
There's no need to cry.

Knock, knock.
Who's there?
Little man.
Little man who?
Little man who can't reach the doorbell.

Knock, knock.
Who's there?
Doris.
Doris who?
Doris jammed; let me in.

Knock, knock.
Who's there?
Ken.
Ken who?
Ken I can come in?

Knock, knock.
Who's there?
Mary.
Mary who?
Mary Christmas.

Knock, knock.
Who's there?
Felix.
Felix who?
Felix my lolly; I'll punch him on the nose.

Knock, knock.
Who's there?
Affro.
Affro who?
Affroed my ball into your garden.

Knock, knock.
Who's there?
Snow.
Snow who?
Snow good asking me.

Knock, knock.
Who's there?
Harry.
Harry who?
Harry up and open the door.

Knock, knock.
Who's there?
Canoe.
Canoe who?
Canoe come out and play today?

Knock, knock.
Who's there?
Ernie.
Ernie who?
Ernie old rags or bones?

Knock, knock.
Who's there?
Wooden shoe.
Wooden shoe who?
Wooden shoe like to know?

Knock, knock.
Who's there?
Dismay.
Dismay who?
Dismay be a joke but it doesn't make me laugh.

Knock, knock.
Who's there?
Amanda.
Amanda who?
Amanda fix the television.

Knock, knock.
Who's there?
Marcella.
Marcella who?
Marcella's full of water, so can you call a plumber?

Knock, knock.
Who's there?
Stan.
Stan who?
Stan back; I'm breaking the door down.

Knock, knock.
Who's there?
A lady with a pram.
Tell her to push off.

Knock, knock.
Who's there?
Phyllis.
Phyllis who?
Phyllis bucket of water, please.

Knock, knock.
Who's there?
Anna.
Anna who?
Annanother thing, how long do I have to keep knocking?

Knock, knock.
Who's there?
Granny.
Granny who?
Knock, knock.
Who's there?
Granny.
Granny who?
Knock, knock.
Who's there?
Auntie.
Auntie who?
Auntie glad Granny's gone?

Knock, knock.
Who's there?
Adolf.
Adolf who?
Adolf ball hid me in de moud and I cand dalk prober dow.

Knock, knock.
Who's there?
A man with a wooden leg.
Tell him to hop it.

Knock, knock.
Who's there?
Cook.
Cook who?
That's the first one I've heard this year.

Knock, knock.
Who's there?
Atch.
Atch who?
Bless you.

MEMORY TEST

Will you remember me for a day?
Yes.
Will you remember me for two days?
Yes.
Will you remember me for a week?
Yes.
Will you remember me for a year?
Yes.
Will you remember me for ten years?
Yes.
Knock, knock.
Who's there?
See, you've forgotten me already!

CROSS-WORDS

What do you get if you cross a pig with a fir tree?
A pork-u-pine.

What do you get if you cross an American president with a shark?
Jaws Washington.

What do you get if you cross a skunk with a bear?
Winnie the Pooh.

What do you get if you cross a frog with a dog?
A croaker spaniel.

What do you get if you cross a kangaroo with a sheep?
A woolly jumper.

What do you get if you cross an elephant with a skunk?
A big stinker.

WHAT A LAUGH!

Wife: (*shaking her husband*): "Wake up! Wake up! There's a burglar in the kitchen and he's eating the stew left over from supper!"
Husband: "Go back to sleep. I'll bury him in the morning."

Manager: "That's the third time you've been late for work this week, Jenkins. Why don't you buy an alarm clock?"
Jenkins: "I've got one, Sir, but it keeps going off while I'm asleep."

A woman phoned an airline in New York to ask how long it would take to fly to San Francisco.

"Just a minute," said a voice.

"Thank you," replied the lady and put the phone down.

Once there was a hen that laid ten eggs. One by one, nine of them hatched into baby chicks. But in the last egg was a pot of marmalade. All the little chicks looked at it and cried, "Oh, look what Mama laid!"

Two eggs were boiling in a saucepan on the stove. One said to the other one, "Cor, I can't stand the heat in here!"

The other one replied, "Wait until you get outside; they'll smash your head in!"

When the dustman called at a house he found that the occupier had forgotten to put his bin outside. So the dustman rang the bell and banged on the door. Eventually, an upstairs window opened and a sleepy head looked out.

"Where's yer bin?" called the dustman.

"I bin asleep," came the answer. "Where's you bin?"

A man poked his head around the betting shop door and asked, "Can I back a horse in here?"

"Yes, Mate," the bookie told him.
"Come on, Black Beauty!" called the man. "Mind the step as you come in!"

Girl: "What nationality are you?"
Friend: "Well, my mother was born in Iceland and my father was born in Cuba, so I guess that makes me an ice cube."

Aunt Mary (*knitting*): "Did you know it takes three sheep to make a jumper?"
Annabel: "I didn't know sheep could knit."

Show-Off: ". . . and so I just leapt out of bed, grabbed my gun and shot the tiger in my pyjamas."
Clever Dick: "Goodness me, what was a tiger doing in your pyjamas?"

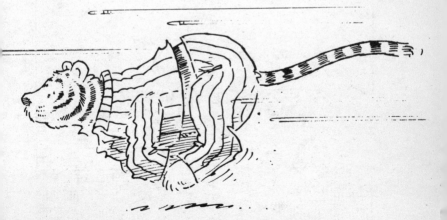

An Irishman, Englishman and Chinaman were all in a hot-air balloon, drinking tea from china cups. As they passed over Ireland, the Irishman looked out and said, "There goes Ireland."

Next, they passed over England and the Englishman leaned out and said, "There goes England."

Then the Chinaman leaned out, dropped his china cup and shouted, "There goes China!"

ANIMAL CRACKERS

What keys are furry?
Monkeys.

Baby Cobra: "Mummy, are we poisonous snakes?"
Mummy Cobra: "Yes, dear. Why?"
Baby Cobra: "I've just bitten my tongue!"

What dog goes into a corner every time the doorbell rings?
A boxer.

How do you make a glow-worm happy?
Cut off his tail and he'll be de-lighted.

Which animals need oiling?
Mice–they squeak.

What's the first thing a bat learns at school?
The alphabat.

What was the sparrow doing in the library?
Looking for some bookworms.

What do mice have that no other animal has?
Baby mice.

What does a hedgehog eat for lunch?
Prickled onions.

Why did the mother kangaroo scold her children?
They were eating biscuits in bed.

What's the best way to catch a rabbit?
Lie down and pretend you're a carrot.

What has four legs and a trunk?
A mouse on holiday.

What are horses' favourite exams?
Haylevels.

What did the beaver say to the tree?
It's been nice gnawing you.

How do frogs cross the road?
They follow the Green Cross Toad.

What's a monkey's favourite pop group?
Bananarama.

COPS N' ROBBERS

A lady wearing a bright orange-and-red checked coat was trying to cross a busy road when a policeman came along. "Constable, can you see me across the road?" she asked.
　　The policeman replied, "I could see you a mile away, madam!"

How do you join the police force?
Handcuff them together.

What does an accountant at a police station do?
Count the coppers.

A little old lady was driving along the road and doing her knitting at the same time. Suddenly a police car drove alongside and a policeman leaned out of the window and shouted, "Pull over!"
　　"No," replied the little old lady, "it's a pair of socks for my husband!"

What do you call a flying policeman?
A helicopper.

What did the policeman say when he saw three angels?
"Halo, halo, halo."

Where do policemen live?
999 Letsbe Avenue.

What did the policeman say to his tummy?
"You're under a vest."

How did the Paris police find Quasimodo?
They followed a hunch.

Did you hear about the two robbers who stole a calendar?
They got six months each.

What happens when you dial 666?
A policeman comes along upside-down.

I SAY, I SAY, I SAY...

What sort of ball doesn't bounce?
A snowball.

What is black and white and eats like a horse?
A zebra.

Where do sheep get their hair cut?
At the baa-baa shop.

What do you call a dinosaur at the North Pole?
Lost.

What do you do if a tyrannosaurus sits in front of you at the cinema?
Miss the film.

What animal do you look like when you have a bath?
A little bear.

Why couldn't the orange get up the hill?
It ran out of juice.

Why is a banana like a pullover?
Because it's easy to slip on.

What's black and white and red all over?
A sunburnt penguin.

What's big, grey and wobbles at the knees?
A jellyphant.

What's round, white and laughs a lot?
A tickled onion.

What's orange and sounds like a parrot?
A carrot.

Who delivers presents to baby sharks at Christmas?
Santa Jaws.

What's worse than finding a maggot in an apple?
Finding half a maggot.

Why did the germ cross the microscope?
To get to the other slide.

Why did the man take a ladder to the party?
Because the drinks were on the house.

Why did the bus stop?
Because it saw a zebra crossing.

Why do nuns walk on their heels?
To save their soles.

Why do French people eat snails?
Because they don't like fast food.

What goes HA! HA! BONK!?
A man laughing his head off.

What's white, furry and has a hole in the middle of it?
A polo bear.

What do you do with a blue banana?
Try and cheer it up.

Why did Gran put skates on her rocking chair?
She wanted to rock and roll.

HOW CLEVER ARE YOU?

What has one horn and gives milk?
A milk truck.

Which side of a cup is the handle on?
The outside.

What begins with T, ends with T and is full of T?
A teapot.

What has a bottom at the top?
A leg.

What do you call five bottles of lemonade?
A pop group.

What's the heaviest part of a fish?
Its scales.

Which bird is mechanical?
The crane.

What's the best way to cover a cushion?
Sit on it.

What do you call a man with a spade on his head?
Doug (dug).

What do you call a girl that sets fire to bills?
Bernadette (burn-a-debt).

What do you call a man with a seagull on his head?
Cliff.

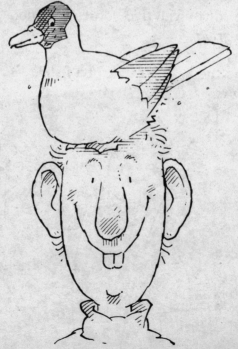

CAN YOU GUESS...?

What happens if you eat yeast and polish?
You rise and shine.

What do you get if you dial 798654301-783645219874873?
A sore finger.

Why are sheep like pubs?
They're full of baas.

Why are false teeth like stars?
They come out at night.

How do you make a sausage roll?
Push it.

How do you keep cool at a football match?
Sit by a fan.

What's the fastest vegetable?
A runner bean.

What goes up and never comes down?
Your age.

Why did the lady have her hair in a bun?
Because her nose was in a burger.

What petrol do snails like?
Shell.

What do toads drink?
Croaker cola.

Where do pigs keep their money?
Piggy banks.

What do you get if you pour hot water down a rabbit hole?
Hot cross bunnies.

BRAINTEASERS

Question: If you put a giraffe, an elephant and a rabbit under an umbrella, which one would get wet?
Answer: None of them. It isn't raining.

Question: There are three shops in the street, a red shop, a blue shop and an orange shop. Which one is the butcher's?
Answer: The one with meat in the window.

Question: A bus full of people was going over Westminster Bridge, but when it got to the other side there wasn't a single person on it. Why?
Answer: They were all married.

Question: If a man was born in England and lived in America all his life, but died on holiday in Spain, where would he be buried?
Answer: In the ground.

Question: What's the quickest way to double your money?
Answer: Fold it in half.

Question: What is as light as a feather but harder to hold?
Answer: Your breath.

Question: What sort of room has no floor, ceiling, windows or door?
Answer: A mushroom.

Question: If two's company and three's a crowd, what are four and five?
Answer: Nine.

WHAT'S THE NAME?

What do you call a wooden king?
A ruler.

What do you call a spy in China?
A Peking Tom.

What do you call a dinosaur with one eye?
Doyouthinkhesaurus?

What do you call a dinosaur with no eyes?
Iknowheneversaurus.

What do you call a deer with no eyes?
No idea.

What do you call a deer with no legs or eyes?
Still no idea.

What do you call a dog with no legs?
You can call it what you want, it still won't come.

What do you call a spider with no legs?
A currant.

What do you call a chick that tells jokes?
A comedihen.

What do you call a high-rise home for pigs?
A styscraper.

What do you call a camel with three humps?
Humphrey.

What do you call a gorilla that swings from cake shop to cake shop?
A meringue-utang.

What do you call two rows of cabbages?
A dual cabbageway.

What do you call a sleeping bull?
A bulldozer.

What do you call a mouse that isn't afraid of a cat?
Lunch.

What do you call Postman Pat without a job?
Pat.

What do you call a snowman with a suntan?
A puddle.

JUMBO JOKES

Why did the elephant leave the circus?
He was tired of working for peanuts.

What time is it when an elephant sits on your fence?
Time to get a new one.

What is big and grey and mutters?
A mumbo jumbo.

What did the man say when he saw a herd of elephants coming over the hill wearing sunglasses?
Nothing. He didn't recognize them.

What is the same size as an elephant, yet weighs nothing?
An elephant's shadow.

How do you stop an elephant from smelling?
Tie a knot in its trunk.

SOMETHING FISHY

What's the most famous fish?
The starfish.

What are the strongest shellfish?
Mussels.

Which fish can sing?
The tuna fish.

Why do so many people like fishing?
It's easy to get hooked.

Why did the fish blush?
It saw the ocean's bottom.

What kind of fish can't swim?
Dead ones.

What do you call a fish with no eyes?
Fsh.

What happened to the stupid jellyfish?
It set.

Which girl would you take fishing with you?
Annette.

Why was the crab arrested?
It kept pinching things.

What sits and shakes at the bottom of the sea?
A nervous wreck.

How does an octopus go to war?
Well armed.

How do a girl and boy octopus go out together?
Hand in hand in hand in hand . . .

What did the sea say to the sand?
Nothing. It just waved.

Why can't you starve on the beach?
Because of all the sand which is there!

IT'S QUACKERS

What happens if ducks fly upside down?
They quack up.

When do ducks get up?
At the quack of dawn.

What do you call a crate of ducks?
A box of quackers.

Why did the man take the duck back to the pet shop?
It had a quack in it.

What do geese watch on TV?
The feather forecast.

DID YOU KNOW...?

Which female singer went for a paddle?
Wet-knee Houston.

What's J.R's favourite sweet?
Ewing gum.

What did Van Gogh say when someone asked him if he wanted a drink?
"No thanks, I've got one ear."

Who sews and eats spinach?
Popeye the tailorman.

What's small, furry and cuts corn?
A combine hamster.

Why do gorillas have big nostrils?
Have you seen the size of their fingers?

What is full of holes but can hold water?
A sponge.

Who always goes to bed with his shoes on?
A horse.

What goes fast and slow?
A tortoise with one pair of roller skates.

What did Batman give Robin for breakfast?
Worms.

What's green and round and good at Kung Fu?
Bruce Pea.

How does a tailor make his trousers last?
He makes the jacket first.

What do you throw to score 100 points on a dartboard?
A porcupine

What can you serve but not eat?
A tennis ball.

CHEEKY KIDS

Mother: "Bobby, did you take a bath this morning?"
Bobby: "No, is one missing?"

Mother: "Did you thank Mrs Smith for inviting you to Jane's party?"
Tina: "No, the girl in front of me thanked her and Mrs Smith said don't mention it, so I didn't."

Angry Mother: "Really, Jimmy, have you been fighting again? How many times have I told you to give and take?"
Jimmy: "I did. I gave him a black eye and took his apple."

Nosy Neighbour: "So your father collects fleas, does he? That's very interesting. And what does your mother do?"
Little Girl: "Scratch."

Mother: "Jackie, go outside, and play with that whistle. Your father can't read the paper."
Jackie: "Cor, I'm only eight and I can read it."

Mother: "Tracy, don't eat off your knife; it's bad manners."
Tracy: "But, Mum, my fork leaks!"

Peter: "Dad, can I have a new pair of trainers for gym?"
Father: "What a cheek! Tell Jim to buy his own trainers."

Mother: "What are you going to take your medicine with today?"
Benny: "A fork!"

Mother: "David, your shoes are on the wrong feet!"
David: "But, Mum, they're the only feet I've got."

Angry Neighbour: "I'll teach you to throw stones at my greenhouse!"
Naughty Boy: "I wish you would. I keep missing!"

Tommy: "Mum, can I keep a skunk under my bed?"
Mother: "What about the smell?"
Tommy: "He'll soon get used to it."

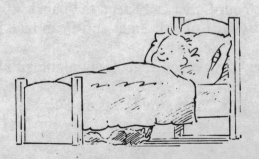

JUNGLE JINKS

What is a zebra?
A horse who can't take off his pyjamas.

What is a crocodile's favourite game?
Snap!

Where does Tarzan get his clothes from?
A jungle sale.

What swings from cake to cake?
Tarzipan.

What do monkeys sing at Christmas?
"Jungle Bells, Jungle Bells . . ."

How do hippos play squash?
They jump on each other.

Why don't leopards ever escape from the zoo?
They are always spotted.

What's a python's favourite game?
Snakes and ladders.

Why can't you pull a snake's leg?
Because he hasn't got one.

Which snakes are good at sums?
Adders.

Why did the egg go into the jungle?
He was an eggsplorer.

What kind of lion never attacks people?
A dandelion.

What do you do if you find a gorilla in your bed?
Sleep somewhere else.

Which football team do snakes support?
Slitherpool.

Why do lions eat raw meat?
Because they don't know how to cook it.

STAN and CLIVE

Clive: "Have you got a hole in your sock?"
Stan: "No."
Clive: "How do you get it on your foot then?"

Clive: "My big brother used to be in the Navy. He worked in submarines but was discharged."
Stan: "Why?"
Clive: "He kept opening the windows to let in some fresh air."

Clive: "Why aren't you eating your hamburger?"
Stan: "I'm waiting for the mustard to cool."

Clive: "How do you keep a twit in suspense?"
Stan: "I don't know."
Clive: "I'll tell you tomorrow."

Clive: "I can turn you into a Red Indian."
Stan: "How?"
Clive: "See."

Clive: "Why are you taking a pencil to bed with you?"
Stan: "So that I can draw the curtains."

Clive: "Do robots have brothers?"
Stan: "No, but they have tran-sisters."

Clive: "Why's that little girl skipping?"
Stan: "She's just taken her medicine and forgotten to shake the bottle."

Clive: "What's the difference between a thought, a fur coat and a monkey?"
Stan: "I don't know."
Clive: "A thought is an idea, a fur coat is too dear and the monkey is you, dear!"

Stan: "Did you hear about the fool who's going around saying No?"
Clive: "No."
Stan: "So it's you, is it?"

INCREDIBLE INSECTS

Where do spiders play football?
At Webley.

What do earwigs sing at football matches?
Earwigo, earwigo, earwigo . . .

Why was the insect kicked out of the park?
Because it was a litterbug.

Which airline do fleas fly on?
British Hairways.

Where do you take a sick wasp?
To the waspital.

What kind of gum do bees chew?
Bumblegum.

Where do you pick up bees?
At a buzz stop.

What's a bee's favourite TV station?
The Bee Bee C.

There were two flies on the wall; which one was a bandit?
The one on the border.

There were two flies in the airing cupboard; which one was Scottish?
The one on the pipes.

SILLY SPORTS

What's an insect's favourite game?
Cricket.

How do you start a flea race?
One, two, flea, go!

How do you start a teddy race?
Ready, teddy, go!

How do you start a pudding race?
Sago.

What dance do two tins do?
The can-can.

If two shirt collars had a race, which one would win?
Neither, it would end in a tie.

Why couldn't the car play football?
Because it didn't have two boots.

Did you hear about the race between the lettuce, the tomato and the tap?
The lettuce was a head, the tap was running and the tomato tried to ketchup.

DOCTOR, DOCTOR...

Patient: "Doctor, Doctor, I feel like the moon."
Doctor: "I can't see you now; you'll have to come back tonight."

Patient: "Doctor, Doctor, I feel like a mirror."
Doctor: "Keep still; I'm trying to comb my hair."

Patient: "Doctor, Doctor, I think I'm turning into a bee."
Doctor: "Buzz off, will you? I'm busy."

Patient: "Doctor, Doctor, I keep thinking I'm a dustbin."
Doctor: "Don't talk rubbish."

Patient: "Doctor, Doctor, I feel like two people."
Doctor: "One at a time, please."

Patient: "Doctor, Doctor, I keep telling lies."
Doctor: "I don't believe you."

Patient: "Doctor, Doctor, I feel like a pair of curtains."
Doctor: "Pull yourself together."

Patient: "Doctor, Doctor, everyone keeps ignoring me."
Doctor: "Next please."

Patient: "Doctor, Doctor, I've only got 59 seconds to live."
Doctor: "Just a minute."

Patient: "Doctor, Doctor, I've got wind."
Doctor: "Buy yourself a kite."

Patient: "Doctor, Doctor, I feel like a needle."
Doctor: "I can see your point."

Patient: "Doctor, Doctor, I can't get to sleep at nights."
Doctor: "Lie on the end of the bed and you'll soon drop off."

Patient: "Doctor, Doctor, I feel like a dog."
Doctor: "Lie down on the couch and I'll examine you."
Patient: "I can't; I'm not allowed on the furniture."

Patient: "Doctor, Doctor, I feel like a bridge."
Doctor: "What's come over you?"
Patient: "So far, a lorry, two buses and three cars."

Patient: "Doctor, Doctor, I feel like an apple."
Doctor: "It's okay; I won't bite you."

Patient: "Doctor, Doctor, I've got flat feet."
Doctor: "Get a foot pump then."

Doctor: "You certainly have acute hearing."
Patient: "Thank you, Doctor. It's real gold, you know."

Patient: "Well, Doctor, what does the x-ray of my brain show?"

Doctor: "Nothing."

Why did the doctor lose his temper?
Because he had no patients.

If an apple a day keeps the doctor away, what does an onion do?
It keeps everyone away.

A man ran into a doctor's surgery, jumped on the doctor and started counting to ten. The doctor pushed him off. "What on earth are you doing?" he demanded.

"Well, I was told I could count on you," replied the man.

QUICK RIDDLES

What did the dentist say when his wife baked a cake?
"I'll do the filling, dear."

What time did the Chinaman go to the dentist?
Tooth hurty.

Why is a rock braver than a mountain?
Because it's a little boulder.

Where should a twenty pound banana go?
On a diet.

What do you do if you find a trumpet growing in your garden?
Root it-oot!

Why can't Cinderella be in the football team?
Because she keeps running away from the ball.

Where will James Bond go when he dies?
Double O's Heaven.

Where did Humpty leave his hat?
Humpty dumped his hat on the wall.

Why did Mickey Mouse go up in space?
To find Pluto.

What kind of shoes are made out of banana skins?
Slippers.

What did the spaceman see in his pan?
An unidentified frying object.

Who gets the sack as soon as he starts work?
The postman.

What do you call a clock in space?
A lunar tick.

What do you find in a wobbly pram?
A jelly baby.

Why did the nurse creep silently past the cupboard?
She didn't want to wake the sleeping pills.

What do people in Scotland eat?
Tart-an-pie.

Which fruit is always on a coin?
A date.

Which fruit is found in a stable?
A strawberry.

What kind of biscuit do you find at the South Pole?
A Penguin.

How do you get down from an elephant?
You don't, you get down from a swan.

Which two things can't you have for breakfast?
Lunch and dinner.

Why did the jelly wobble?
Because it saw the milk shake.

How do you make an apple puff?
Chase it around the garden.

Why are astronauts successful people?
Because they always go up in the world.

What's green and smells?
Kermit's nose.

What's black and white and read all over?
A newspaper.

How does Jack Frost get to work?
By icicle.

What is in steeple but not in church, at the end but not at the start, in the earth but not in the moon?
The letter E.

Where do sheep go for their holidays?
The Baa-haa-maas.

What is black and white and rolls?
A penguin falling down Mount Everest.

What is black and white and laughs?
The zebra that pushed him.

Why is gossip like a kiss?
It passes from mouth to mouth.

Why is 6 afraid of 7?
Because 7 ate 9 (7, 8, 9).

What jumps higher than a house?
You for a start – a house can't jump.

What's green and never stops complaining?
Apple grumble.

HORROR HOWLERS

What sort of ship does Dracula sail on?
A blood vessel.

What do ghost children play?
Haunt and seek.

Why do witches do well at school?
Because they are good at spelling.

What's Dracula's favourite game?
Batminton.

What's a cannibal's favourite game?
Swallow my leader.

What do you call a monster that's kind and handsome?
A failure.

Where are green monsters found?
Green monsters never get lost.

What do ghosts eat for breakfast?
Dreaded wheat.

What do you call a skeleton who won't work?
Lazybones.

What do you take from a witch to make her itch?
W.

What do monsters eat after having their teeth out?
The dentist.

What do you get if you cross an ice cube with a vampire?
Frost bite.

What did the barman say when the ghost asked for a drink?
Sorry, we don't serve spirits.

What do monsters eat at sea?
Fish and ships.

Which monster eats faster than all the other monsters?
The goblin.

What do spooks eat?
Spookhetti on toast.

Why do ghosts make terrible liars?
You can see right through them.

What do ghosts like for dessert?
Ice scream.

What do ghosts like to chew?
Boo-blegum.

What did the daddy ghost say to his son?
I've told you before, only spook when you're spooken to.

Did you hear about the three identical witches?
No one could tell which witch was which!

What do monsters eat for lunch?
Monster Munch.

Why couldn't the skeleton go to the dance?
He had no body to go with.

Where do ghosts go at Christmas?
The phantomime.

What did one ghost say to the other ghost?
Do you believe in people?

What did they call Dracula?
A pain in the neck.

What happened when the two monsters met?
It was love at first fright.

Where do monsters go to get married?
Westmonster Abbey.

How does a monster count to 13?
It uses its fingers.

How does a witch tell the time?
She uses a witchwatch.

SPOT THE DIFFERENCE

What's the difference between a jeweller and a jailor?
One sells watches and the other watches cells.

What's the difference between stork and butter?
Butter can't stand on one leg.

What's the difference between a nail and a boxer?
One gets knocked in and the other gets knocked out.

What's the difference between the letters M.A.K.E.S. and a wizard?
One makes spells and the other spells makes.

What's the difference between a gorilla and a banana?
Have you ever seen a gorilla in a fruit bowl?

MUMMY, MUMMY...

Harry: "Mummy, Mummy, the ladder's fallen down!"
Mother: "I'm busy, go and tell Daddy."
Harry: "He already knows; he was on it!"

Annie: "Mummy, Mummy, why is Daddy running so fast?"
Mother: "Shut up and pass me those bullets."

Jerry: "Mummy, Mummy, I don't want to go to Australia."
Mother: "Shut up and keep digging."

Robin: "Mummy, Mummy, why is Daddy hanging over the cliff?"
Mother: "Shut up and keep jumping on his fingers."

Katie: "Mummy, Mummy, I don't want to go to France."
Mother: "Shut up and keep swimming."

Veronica: "Mummy, Mummy, why can I only go out at night?"
Mother: "Shut up and drink your blood."

FARMYARD FUN

What do you give a pig with a sore throat?
Oinkment.

What sort of sweets do pigs like best?
Swine gums.

Why shouldn't you tell secrets to pigs?
Because they're squealers.

Where do pigs sleep?
In hammocks.

What goes aab, aab?
A backward sheep.

How do sheep keep warm in winter?
By central bleating.

Where do sheep go to get their hair cut?
The baabaa shop.

What's a horse's favourite TV programme?
Neigh-h-h-bours.

Why do hens watch TV?
For hentertainment.

How do chickens dance?
Chick to chick.

On which side has a chicken got more feathers?
On the outside.

Which animals are the most sensible?
Horses because they're stable.

Which animals didn't go into the ark in pairs?
Maggots – they went in apples.

What goes woof woof tick?
A watch dog.

What do you get if you cross a cow, a sheep and a goat?
The milky baa kid.

RIDICULOUS RHYMES

There once was a fat boy called Kid,
Who ate twenty mince pies for a quid.
When asked, "Are you faint?"
He replied, "No, I ain't,
But I don't feel as well as I did."

There was a young lady from Leeds,
Who swallowed a packet of seeds,
Within just one hour,
Her nose was a flower
And her hair was a big bunch of weeds.

Jack and Jill went up the hill,
To fetch a pail of water.
Jack fell down and broke his crown,
And Jill said, "You twit! Now I'll have to fill
the bucket up again!"

There was a young man from Harrow,
Whose nose was too long and too narrow,
It gave him so much trouble,
That he bent it up double,
And wheeled it around in a barrow.

Mary had a little lamb,
It had a touch of colic.
She gave it brandy twice a day,
And now it's alcoholic!

AND FINALLY ...

A man found an elephant walking down the street one day. He took it to the police station and asked, "What shall I do with this elephant?"

"Take it to the zoo," replied the policeman on the desk.

The next day the same policeman saw the same man walking down the street with the elephant.

"I thought I told you to take that elephant to the zoo," said the policeman.

"I did," replied the man, "and today I'm taking it to the pictures."

More hilarious joke books from HIPPO . . .

The Skeleton in the Cupboard Joke Book *by Josh and Jake Alverson*
You'll scream with laughter at all the rattling good jokes in this hilarious book of hallowe'en howlers. It's rib-tickling good fun!

The Noah's Ark Joke Book *by Olive Branch*
You'll find floods of porcupine puns, trunkloads of elephant jokes and hundreds of hippo howlers in this bumper joke book all about Noah's Ark.

The School Joke Book *by Susannah Bradley*
Here's a joke book with a difference. It's huge and it's full of pictures! There's a joke for every school occasion – in the classroom, in the cloakroom, in the toilets, behind the bike sheds . . . – and they're all told by a bunch of crazy cartoon kids! Even the most boring teacher will roar with laughter!

The Cops 'n' Robbers Joke Book *by Laura Norder*
Did you ever read a book with a police siren on the top? Well, now's your chance . . .

Follow the antics of Burglar Bill, Smasher Smith and Sneaky Sid as they try to escape the clutches of Detective Golightly, P.C. Pouncer and W.P.C. Perfect (not forgetting Woofer, the police dog). It's packed with hundreds of hilarious cops 'n' robbers jokes.